AF225801

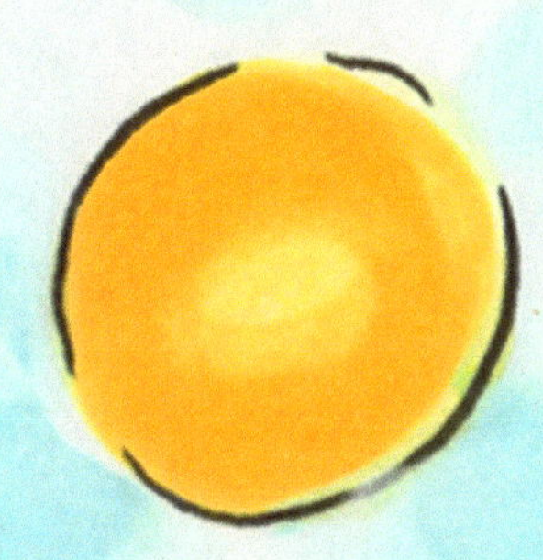

Flight *of the* Headless Chicken

~

Can living from the **heart**
give chickens wings that work?

Story by Ben Slager ، Pictures by Paige Rohrick

Copyright © 2015 Ben Slager

All rights reserved. No part of this publication may be reproduced or transmitted in any form or by any mechanical, photographic, or electronic means, including photocopying, recording, or by any information storage and retrieval system now known or to be invented, without permission in writing from the publisher.

Printed in the USA

Illustrations by Paige Rohrick
Book design by Fiona Raven

Published by Out of the Box Press
a division of BMEC Mindful Enterprises Corporation

Library and Archives Canada Cataloguing in Publication

Slager, Ben, 1970–, author
Flight of the headless chicken : can living from the heart give chickens wings that work? / story by Ben Slager ; pictures by Paige Rohrick.

ISBN 978-0-9939499-0-6 (BOUND)
ISBN 978-0-9939499-1-3 (PBK.)

I. Rohrick, Paige, 1994–, illustrator II. Title.

PS8637.L35F55 2014 JC811'.6 C2014-907410-7

fothc.com

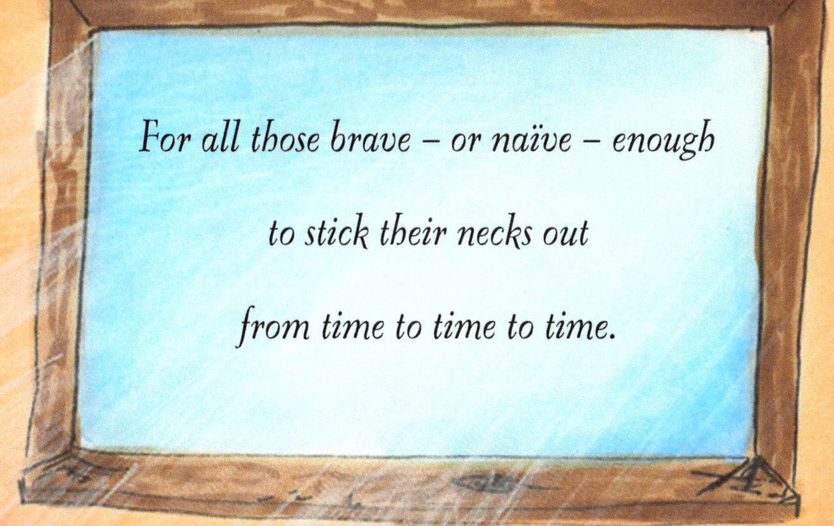
For all those brave – or naïve – enough
to stick their necks out
from time to time to time.

Once upon a time –

– a time beaten by a stick upon a different and daring drum –
There was a particularly *plucky* chicken who
Fouled up a farmer's main course
And who, in *not* being had for Sunday dinner,
Found some *fantastical-fanatical*
         good fun!

You see, this freaky fowl clearly lost her head –
In fact – she lost it *through and through*!
At the sure and steady hand of a farmer
who did, well,
What farming folks do do.

It was in an unthinking blink of *wide-chicken-eyed* excitement
That this bird-brain stuck her neck out –

And farmer *grabbed-her-nabbed-her* –
Fearful-frantic – from the huddled flock –

And with a flash of his *stainless-steely-sharp* hatchet +
The age-old act   was done
on his well-worn butcher's block.

But she . . . this *chickadee* . . . was not quite, not *fully* dead –

And off she sprung with spring –

Chicken feet, chicken legs, chicken breast –

But no chicken head!!!

Yes off she – well, *most* of she – *scrambled*
Past the collie, the crows, the cows and the old, proud cock,
And past the tidy farmhouse where the plate-proud farmer's wife
Was baking fresh bread and thickening her stock.

Through the clean, lined laundry,
Across the farmer's field, so prudently plowed
Headily-heedlessly under the nose of the dumb-founded forest fox
Left pondering and perplexed – *befuddled-muddled* – in a cloud.

Blissfully-blindly bang into the butt of another land-locked,
Big-breasted bird, with *its* head firmly stuck in the sand,
Leaving the bewildered farmer far, far behind, mouth open
Hatchet raised and tightly gripped in his still-trembling hand.

Truly, *actually*, like a chicken with its head cut off,
Poultry in motion, on and on did the inspired head-and-cage freed bird run
Free range through dark valleys and up happy hills
Minding nothing in her way – meddling with no one.

Quickly past Chicken Little – she frantic and head covered
Screeching-preaching to all that the sky was falling still,
And easily – if not gingerly – past the Gingerbread Man –

he running *Kooky-cutter-crazily* –

but not fast enough
for his dangerously proud will.

Swiftly on by the pen of the Little Red Hen,
She *talk-squawking* her little head off while *hustling-rustling* up stores of grain
Twisting and turning in a foul and *frustrated-frenzied* muss of fuss,
As if captive in an ironclad, barn-perched, weather vane.

Then *hastily-happily* up to a pony-tailed girl crouched, alone, on a bus bench
Her head and spirit bowed low, sending yet another text ☹
Imagine the sparkle in this girl's big blue eyes if she'd only looked up to see
The *amazing-alarming-awe-inspiring* spectacle coming by next! :o

Pitter-patter-patter-pitter our headless bird's tough little die-hard
Chicken legs did, indeed, make a trek of it;
All her eggs in one basket, playing chicken with the troubles on her path,
   counting her chickens before they were hatched and
Crossing the road why? Well . . . just for the *heck* of it! ☺

Until, specially and wonderfully seasoned,

her feathered form slowly,

inevitably, fatigued and fumbled . . .

. . . and into the soft, lush grasses

along the side of the winding road . . .

this chicken – faint – but *not* faint of *heart* –

finally tumbled. . . .

. . . gently . . . slowly . . .

into the deep, sweet sleep

of happy story-book ends,

drifting away

in the winged arms of beaming,

white-feathered family,

and beaming,

white-feathered

friends. . . .

And her very last words, *chicken-scratched* in the dust,

but if she'd had her head, she no doubt would have said:

fothc.com